IMPERIAL ROME AT WAR

Text by MARTIN WINI

Colour plates by ANG

Copyright © 1996
by CONCORD PUBLICATIONS CO.
603-609 Castle Peak Road
Kong Nam Industrial Building
10/F, B1, Tsuen Wan
New Territories, Hong Kong

We welcome authors who can help
expand our range of books. If you
would like to submit material, please
feel free to contact us.

We are always on the look-out for new,
unpublished photos for this series.
If you have photos or slides or
information you feel may be useful to
future volumes, please send them to us
for possible future publication.
Full photo credits will be given upon
publication.

ISBN 962-361-608-2
Printed in Hong Kong

The armies of Imperial Rome, and the 500-year history of the empire which they won and defended, are the shared foundation of the whole Western military tradition.

There is no simple explanation for the access of vigour through which a nation rises to seize its historical hour of dominance; we can never know "why", but can sometimes puzzle over the "how". In the 8th Century BC Rome was an obscure village guarding a river crossing in north-east Italy. She threw off Etruscan rule in the 6th Century, and herself dominated the whole Italian peninsula by the mid-3rd Century. Between the 60s and 140s BC she destroyed the great western Mediterranean empire of Carthage, and came to dominate Greece, Asia Minor and Egypt. By 120 AD Rome's rule extended from the Atlantic almost to the Caspian, from northern England to southern Iraq. Despite catastrophic setbacks she remained the single strongest power in the Western world, and its only "modern" military machine, until the early 5th Century AD. She achieved this record, unique in history, with an army which until the 4th Century never exceeded about 320,000 infantry and 30,000 cavalry.

We have no scope here to do more than touch briefly upon the organisation and character of that army; but its essential differences from those of the other peoples of the day are simply stated. The Roman legionary was the first *soldier* in Western history, and the only true soldier in a world of warriors or, at best, short-term mercenaries. He was a professional, long-service infantryman, paid wages by the state; and serving that state, wherever it sent him, in the ranks of permanent tactical units of uniform strength and organisation. He received uniform armour, field equipment and weapons, and was uniformly trained in their use. He was led by professional officers following a uniform career structure - the centurions, that unique pool of fighting men who provided Rome with her invaluable continuity of experienced combat leadership.

The legionary was the luxury afforded by an enormously rich mercantile state, whose centralised, bureaucratic government invested its surplus revenues in a military machine designed to increase its territory and wealth. The legionary's enemies were, almost invariably, tribal warriors - pastoral or agricultural peoples for whom warfare could only be intermittent. They had no command structure or culture of discipline beyond temporary personal loyalty to a chieftain; no state resources, and thus no consistent standard of equipment or functioning logistics; no systematic tactical training; no systems of communication or co-ordinated control. Personal courage, strength and numbers could not outweigh these handicaps when faced by a professional army fighting under circumstances of its own choosing. The legions did not always enjoy this choice, however; and from the 3rd Century onwards they were increasingly forced to respond to the enemy's initiative, with increasingly dispiriting results.

We choose to limit the scope of this book to the period from the mid-1st Century BC (before which we have too little evidence to even attempt realistic reconstructions), until the late 4th Century AD (after which the character of the Imperial army, already degraded, changed out of all recognition).

The Legion

The essential background to understanding the commentaries on the individual plates is the basic nature of the Roman legion.

The army of the Republic, up to the late 2nd Century BC, was raised annually, partly by a levy of Roman citizens meeting a minimum property qualification, and partly from allied peoples fulfilling treaty obligations. The citizen levy was organised in "legions" - units between 4,000 and 5,000 strong. Each was divided internally, by age and standard of equipment, into three classes of heavy infantry and a fourth class of light skirmishers, plus some 300 aristocratic cavalry. Each legion was also divided into 60 tactical sub-units or "centuries", led by elected officers - "centurions"; two centuries formed a "maniple".

Citizen levies, enlisted temporarily and providing their own equipment, served Rome's needs for short local campaigns; but not for aggressive wars of expansion, or for establishing garrisons, on distant fronts. From about 100 BC the dictator Gaius Marius began a major programme of reforms; these led directly to the very different army organised by the first emperor, Augustus Caesar, in the aftermath of the long civil wars from which he emerged supreme in 30 AD.

The early Imperial legion was nominally some 5,500 strong, composed of a single class of heavy armoured infantrymen (apart from 120 cavalry scouts and messengers). It was divided into ten "cohorts" about 480 strong, each of six centuries of about 80 men; from the mid-1st Century AD the elite First Cohort in each legion was increased to around 800 men in five double-size centuries. Centuries and cohorts were led by centurions, now promoted from the ranks on merit.

The legionary recruit had to be a citizen - a civic status steadily extended outwards from the heartland to embrace first all Italians, and later men from various provinces of the empire. He signed on for 25 years' salaried service, with the hope of bonuses marking important victories, the accession of a new emperor, etc.; and the promise of a generous discharge gratuity or land grant. These land grants were made in "colonies", settlements planted in the provinces, to increase the Romanisation of the empire. The army became an attractive career for the poorer classes of Italy and, later, the older provinces such as Gaul, Spain, Dalmatia, etc.

Under Augustus there were initially 28 legions; some were wiped out, some disbanded in disgrace, some raised as replacements, but the usual number at any period was around 30 - never more than 33 or less than 25. Each legion had a number, and many had names - recalling the emperor who raised them, regions where they had been raised or had served, or various honorifics; extra titles were sometimes added to honour distinguished service, e.g. *Martia Victrix*, "victorious in war". Because Augustus's army was formed from the contending civil war armies the numbers were often duplicated: e.g. there were three distinct "Third Legions" - *III Augusta*, *III Gallica* and *III Cyrenaica*. Several legions were named *Gemina* "twinned", indicating amalgamation of two earlier legions; other notable titles include *Legio VI Ferrata* (roughly, "the iron legion"), and *Legio XII Fulminata* (roughly, "the lightning-bolts").

At around the end of the chaotic 3rd Century the classic legions seem largely to have been broken up, rationalising the practical results of years of improvisation under pressure. Many "vexillations" - detachments - had been stripped away from the legions based around the frontiers, to support the claims of pretenders to the throne or to resist attacks on other provinces, often never to return. Both the much weakened rump legions and their distant detachments - averaging perhaps 1,000 men - seem to have been given formal identity "in place" as legions, many serving henceforward with the new mobile field armies.

The Evidence

The reconstructions shown in this book are based upon the standard interpretations of various types of evidence - sculptures, mosaics and wall-paintings; archaeological finds; and written sources. The reader must always bear in mind, however, that surviving evidence is sparse, fragmentary, and seldom closely datable; it usually lacks context, and its interpretation even by the most scholarly authorities is often little more than educated guesswork. The subject of the Imperial Roman army - like all ancient history - is like a jigsaw puzzle with a thousand pieces; we have found ten or twenty pieces, one or two of which seem to fit together, here and there - but the exact context of most of our individual discoveries remains more or less mysterious.

Legionaries of Caesar's army in action in central Gaul, c.52 BC

Plate 1

During the 50s BC the political adventurer G.Julius Caesar, entrusted by the Senate with command of an army of up to 11 legions, proved himself a brilliant and ruthless general in a series of almost genocidal victories over the unruly tribes of central and northern Gaul (modern France and Belgium).

Roman infantry tactics seem to have been fairly straightforward; they were successful because they were co-ordinated, under central command, by drilled and disciplined soldiers. Most of their enemies were strong, brave, but individualistic warriors who lacked any effective command and control, or any culture of co-ordinated obedience. They were therefore vulnerable to confusion, and seldom able to react quickly to changing circumstances.

The legionaries fought in blocks of sub-units, the basic block apparently a pair of centuries (the "maniple"), the sub-units drawn up in three distinct lines. As the first line advanced to the attack the front few ranks threw *pila*- javelins with long iron shanks, which bent or broke from the shaft on impact and could not be thrown back. They then closed with the enemy in tight ranks, semi-crouching, left shoulders braced against their shields, protected against downward blows by their helmets and mailed shoulders, on their blind side and against spear thrusts by their shields - which could also be used to hit and shove. Their enemies typically used slashing weapons of soft iron; the legionary stabbed upwards round the edge of his shield with the point of his short Spanish- style *gladius* sword (though its edge was also deadly - we read of severed arms and heads).

Legionaries were drilled to change their frontage in battle as events dictated, with rear sub-units moving out and forward to double the line; or contracting the line by falling back and inwards into deeper blocks. Most critically, however, they were trained to relieve one another after a few moments' fighting, by ranks within the maniple and by units. At the signal - presumably a trumpet call - the units engaged would temporarily contract or open up lanes in their frontage,

the next line pressing forward between them: exact deta[ils] are unknown, but the effect was certainly that tired men fe[ll] back and fresh men stepped forward into their places. Th[is] manoeuvre alone - requiring impressive discipline confidence and timing when in hand-to-hand combat multiplied their effective strength, against a compacte[d] enemy mass whose (rapidly tiring) front edge alone cou[ld] actually bring weapons to bear.

Here a unit of Julius Caesar's army fight off a Gallic sort[ie] against their siege works. The front rank tires; a centuric[n] shouts for relief, and the next rank move up to throw javelir[s] over their comrades' heads, to win a moment's respite for th[e] change-over. Evidence for the equipment of Julian peric[d] legionaries is very scarce; it suggests an evolved combinatic[n] of Graeco-Etruscan and Celtic styles. Celtic-style ringmc[il] shirts had doubled shoulder reinforcements, sometime[s] decorated in Greek fashion; plumed bronze helmets were [of] so-called "Montefortino" shape, tall-domed wi[th] shortneckguards and large cheekguards; the big plywoc[d] *scutum* shield, with a central spine and boss, was of "wra[p] around" oval shape; the *gladius* had a broad-shouldere[d] blade with a long tapering point.

Traditionally, legionaries are depicted in red tunics; in fac[t] recent analysis of the sparse evidence strongly suggests th[at] white was the usual colour, with centurions perhaps wearir[g] red - this latter is little more than guesswork, but we choose [to] follow it throughout most of these plates.

Ambush in the Teutoburg Forest, 9 AD

Plate 2

In 31 BC his kinsman Octavianus emerged as unchallenged victor of the long civil wars which followed the assassination of the dictator Julius Caesar; and in 27 BC he took the title Augustus, becoming in fact if not in name the first emperor. His reign saw his soldier stepsons Drusus and Tiberius (his heir) succeed him in leading vigorous campaigns of imperial expansion - and crushing the many consequent and bitter uprisings - in Spain, the Alps, the Balkans, Hungary and Germany.

Marius's reforms a hundred years before had turned the legion into a uniformly equipped brigade of heavy infantry at the cost of stripping it of its previously integral light skirmisher and cavalry elements. These necessary "auxiliary" troops were now hired *en masse* for particular campaigns from among border peoples; led by their own chiefs, who were given Roman officer status, they provided their own weapons and gear - but they took home with them more knowledge of the Roman army than was always wise.

Augustus seems to have planned final north-eastern frontiers on the River Elbe and the Carpathians, well beyond the Rhine and Danube, and many German tribes submitted to client status in 11-9 BC. But their resistance was far from broken; and in 9 AD three Roman legions under Quinctilius Varus suffered catastrophic defeat somewhere near modern Osnabruck at the hands of Cherusci tribesmen from the Weser basin, led by a chief and former auxiliary officer named Arminius.

After a season's campaigning towards the Elbe Varus was lured, in wet autumn weather, into the forbidding maze of the Teutoburg Forest. On narrow paths through primeval swamp-forest the Romans' normally sophisticated column of march broke down; when they were exhausted and disoriented their treacherous guides, and many local *auxilia* who were supposedly guarding flanks and rear, turned on them at the head of the tribesmen lurking in ambush. In thick woodland, unable to form ranks properly for battle and attacked from all sides, the army was broken up and hunted to destruction in a wretched running fight. *Legio XVII, XVIII* and *XIX* were wiped out, the wounded and captured dragged away to hideou deaths or lifelong slavery; Varus preferred suicide on the fie to death by torture. In one battle Rome suffered th destruction of 12 per cent of her professional army, a seriou blow to her confidence, and the encouragement of all he other enemies and restless subjects. Never again wou Romans try to conquer Germany; the Rhine valley remaine the frontier - periodically threatened by tribal pressure fro the east.

The Augustan legionary's kit had changed in small b noticeable ways over the last 50 years. Gallic helmet type had been taken into use and developed. The left and cent legionaries here wear the simple low-domed bron "Coolus", shaped rather like a reversed jockey cap, with small flat neckguard and added browguard. The veterc selling his life dearly with his *dolabra* pickaxe has one of th first models of the splendid headpiece called by historia "Imperial Gallic" (compare with Gallic chief in centre of Pla 1), which would be perfected in Rhineland smithies over th next century or more. Over their ringmail legionaries now wo two crossed, metal-plated belts supporting the sword on th right hip (an inexplicably awkward position for drawing, b retained for another 200 years), and a dagger on the left. T plywood shield, protected by a leather cover on the marc was now of "wrap-around clipped oval" shape, cut straig at the top and bottom; it would soon be seen alongside th more familiar "wrap-around rectangular" type.

Legio XIIII make an opposed landing on Anglesey, c.60 AD

Plate 3

Nearly 20 years after the Emperor Claudius ordered the invasion of Britain in 43 AD, the north-western half of the island remained free. Nero's reign saw the governor Suetonius Paulinus campaigning against the hill tribes of Wales, climaxing in a crossing of the Menai Strait to storm Anglesey island, the stubbornly-defended holy place of the Druidic cult. With proper planning and preparation the legions and auxiliaries could successfully carry out even such a perilous operation as an opposed beach landing - though if caught in the open on the march by superior numbers they remained vulnerable.

With *Legio XIIII Gemina* and *XX Valeria* far off in Wales, Queen Boudicca of the Iceni tribe led a mass uprising in East Anglia which wiped out a large part of *Legio IX Hispana* on the march. The tribes destroyed Colchester and London, nearly forcing the abandonment of Britain before the *Gemina* and *Valeria* won a final desperate victory near St.Albans in 61 AD.

Here legionaries hurl their *pila* javelins (note this lead-weighted version, left) as they wade ashore. They wear the new articulated plate cuirass (today called the "Corbridge" type, after a famous archaeological find). Though probably far from general issue yet, fragmentary finds prove it was worn fairly early in the British campaigns.

This ingenious *lorica segmentata* was presumably adopted to give better protection when fighting tall Western Celtic tribesmen using long slashing swords. Of 40 separate smoothly overlapping iron plates rivetted to internal strapping, it was flexible and well-balanced (though the flimsy hinges often broke, and the neck plates fitted uncomfortably).

Tombstones show centurions and standard-bearers (left and right background) retaining ringmail or scale armour. Centurions also wore greaves; and transverse crests - note his "Imperial Gallic" helmet, now fully developed into a handsome, enveloping design with a deep neckguard, often decorated with bronze bosses and reeding, and interestingly

retaining the embossed "eyebrows" of its Celtic model. Unlik[e] legionaries, centurions wore their swords on the left; all swor[d] - by now the parallel-sided "Pompeii" model with a short poi[nt] - were slung from baldrics. A single waistbelt supported [a] dagger, and for legionaries a groin-apron of studded strap[s;] surviving decorated weapons and fittings show that soldie[rs] enjoyed freedom to display their relative wealth by th[e] quality of their kit.

The *signifer*, wearing a bear's pelt over his special helm[et] with a pointed peak (and a detachable full-face metal ma[sk] for parades), earned double pay as the senior of th[e] century's three "NCOs"; the others were the *optio* (see Pla[te] 4), and the *tesserarius*, perhaps an "orderly sergean[t."] Standards were venerated, and their bearers risked their liv[es] in the forefront of battle to inspire the troops. No standar[d] bearer is listed at cohort level (though the cohort may ha[ve] had other kinds of insignia); most known examples bear fr[om] one to six metal discs - presumably the century's numb[er] within the cohort - and other decorations, like this Capric[orn] image, perhaps an emperor's Zodiacal sign.

We copy this *signum* from the tombstone of a *signifer* [of] *Legio XIIII*; and from another the shield blazon, the only o[ne] clearly identified to a specific unit - there is evidence th[at] legions bore identifying shield blazons, though colours [are] guesswork. *Signifers* are shown with oval or round shie[lds] smaller than the wrap-around rectangular or "clipped ov[al"] *scutum* shown carried by legionaries.

8

Legionaries assault a Judaean city, c.67 AD

Plate 4

Judaea (modern Israel) had become a Roman client state in Augustus's reign; seized as a province by Claudius, it was always prone to rebellion. Between c.66 and 73 AD a large Roman army was engaged against Jewish patriot forces; initially under the able general Vespasianus, it was later led - when he made his successful bid for the throne in 69 - by his son Titus. This long, savage war involved the siege and storming of several walled cities and other strongholds; the battles for Jerusalem and Masada are well-known epics.

Rome's expertise in siege warfare - based directly on much older Greek equipment and methods - far outclassed that of any enemy (except perhaps the Sassanid Persians) that she ever fought. The assembly of huge amounts of material; the methodical construction, by thousands of men, of vast works - surrounding ramparts, mines under walls, mobile galleries and battering rams, towers, approach ramps; the steady contraction, over months or even years; the final assault, and pitiless massacre - this type of operation suited the Roman character perfectly, and was virtually irresistible.

"Artillery" was issued to each legion: one light arrow-shooting "scorpion" per century, and one heavy stone-throwing *ballista* per cohort, giving the legion some 70 catapults of a range of sizes - the measurement determining "calibre" was the diameter of the bronze washers clamping the ends of the twisted sinew or hair springs in which the arms of these giant crossbows were set. Artillery was massed together to lay down "battery fire" (for both sieges and open-field battles). The *ballistae* threw stones of anything between 2lbs. and a massive 60lbs. weight out to at least 150 yards; while they battered the walls, the heavy wooden-flighted *scorpio* bolts swept defenders off the ramparts from up to 300 yards' range.

Here a *scorpio* crew reload at the critical moment, to "shoot in" an assault party charging a breach in the famous locked-shields *testudo* formation used for advancing inside the range of enemy missiles. One man winds back the sliding bolt-trough with the bowstring clamped to its rocking trigger

mechanism. His helmet is a so-called "Imperial Italic" type, often of bronze, and of poorer quality than the "Imperial Gallic" types, it generally resembles them except in lacking their characteristic "eyebrow" embossing and in having round, slotted crest fixture. It had been thought that the articulated plate cuirass was not used in the East (where legionaries did not face tall Celtic enemies with long slashing swords), until fragments were found at Gamala in Israel, contemporary battle site. Both ringmail and bronze or tinned scale armour were certainly still worn by some legionaries the 60s - as were old-fashioned helmets like the "jockey cap" worn by the soldier shouting for more ammunition.

Beyond the crew an *optio*, the centurion's second-in command in each century, is identified by his helmet side plumes and long knobbed staff. These "NCOs" received at least half again, and perhaps double, a legionary's annual pay of 225 silver *denarii*. Soldiers of this period were paid three times a year; in the 80s Domitianus increased the rate to 30 *denarii* paid in four instalments - though soldiers actual received much less, after "deductions at source" against the cost of food, weapons, kit replacement, compulsory payments towards burial clubs and various other unit funds. The century standard-bearer also supervised the banking part of a legionary's pay against his retirement.

Auxiliary cavalry raid on German village, c.83 AD

Plate 5

Although the Varus disaster effectively ended Roman ambitions to occupy Germany beyond a narrow buffer zone east of the Rhine, there were many later campaigns involving temporary thrusts into "free Germany". The reign of Domitianus saw fierce fighting in the Taunus hills against the Chatti tribe of, roughly, modern Hesse-Cassel; such campaigns were ruthlessly pursued, with fast-moving columns destroying tribal villages and food resources.

By this period most auxiliaries served in regular units organised on Roman lines under Roman and provincial officers. Recruited for 25 years' service from among non-citizens, and paid less than legionaries, auxiliaries received on discharge the important privilege of citizenship for themselves and their descendants. The elite were the cavalry *alae* ("wings"); Rome, having no cavalry traditions, always employed troopers from horse-breeding areas such as Spain, Gaul, Thrace and North Africa. The usual *ala quingenaria* seems to have had about 500 men in 16 *turmae* (troops) of about 32 men; by about 110 AD there were some 75 of these regiments. From the mid-1st century AD a few crack *alae milliariae* were added - only nine are known, never more than one stationed in any province - comprising 24 troops, about 800 men.

Alae bore numbers and/or names referring to the peoples from whom they were raised, and sometimes the emperor at the time of raising; a few kept the name of their first commander; brave or loyal service could add further conventional phrases, until the title became long and complex. A simple example was *Ala I Augusta Thracum* ("1st Thracian Horse, raised under Augustus"); but the elite unit in Britain was the *Ala Augusta Gallorum Petriana milliaria civium Romanorum bis torquata* ("Petrus's Gallic Horse, raised under Augustus, a thousand strong, awarded block Roman citizenship, twice decorated"). The unit standard was a *vexillum*, a flag on a staff and crossbar.

Horses were small, mostly 13 or 14 hands high, probably ungelded stallions; note here simple geometric brands on shoulder and rump. Snaffle and curb bits and hackamore have been found, as have prick-spurs. The saddle, copie from a Gallic Celtic model, had four bronze-stiffened horn despite the lack of stirrups experiments show that it gav enough support for thrusts and blows with spear and swor Tombstones show troopers with oval or hexagonal shiel stabbing overarm or thrusting underarm with a short lance. description survives of training with javelins, the troopers ridir in sequence and throwing several at a target befor wheeling away; there is mention of a quiver to carry thes and we reconstruct it here in a logical position. The caval sword, *spatha*, resembled the legionary's *gladius* but was u to three feet long.

Ringmail and scale cuirasses are shown in sculptures, th former often with Celtic-style reinforcing capes, or shoulde doublings as in Plates 1-3; one carving (see backgroun figure) even shows a ringmail shirt worn with the upper sectic of a legionary *lorica segmentata* reinforcing the vulnerab shoulders. Carvings show calf-length breeches worn benea the tunic. Recovered and carved cavalry helmets basica resemble the legionary shape, but without browguards; wi cheekguards covering the ears; and very often with more less elaborate decorative chasing, silver-gilt skinnin medallions, etc. - locks of "hair" over the skull were popul Owners' inscriptions scratched on some suggest th although elaborate, these were not officers' helmets.

A Praetorian Cohort on the Danube front, c.88 AD

Plate 6

In 85-88 AD several costly campaigns on the Danube front occupied the Emperor Domitianus; the Dacians (from modern Transylvania) overran the province of Moesia (roughly, northern Bulgaria/eastern Yugoslavia), inflicting heavy losses before his legions drove them back. He was accompanied at the front by part of the Praetorian Guard - the elite bodyguard force (then of ten large ten-century cohorts) normally stationed in Rome.

The Praetorians, recruited in Italy, enjoyed many privileges: three times a legionary's pay; nearly twice his discharge gratuity after only 16 (instead of 25) years' service, spent mostly in the comfort of the capital; excellent career prospects - and occasional huge bonuses given by a new or reigning emperor to buy the Praetorians' loyalty. They understood their power to create or destroy emperors, and sometimes used it frivolously, with damaging consequences for Rome.

Here the tribune commanding a Praetorian Cohort receives a despatch from one of the Guard's cavalry component - apparently, 150 men within each 800-strong cohort. Guard tribunes were former centurions - more experienced than men of the same rank on a legion's staff, who might only have four years' service. His purple-striped tunic marks his rank; we choose to show a red cloak, perhaps from his days as a frontier centurion. Senior officers are always sculpted wearing the moulded or "muscle" cuirass copied from the ancient Greek model, over decorated protective straps (*pteruges*) hanging from a jerkin beneath the armour, and half-breeches. No surviving example of this "Attic" style helmet (beloved of Hollywood!) has been recovered, and its illustration is pure guesswork; but it often appears in sculpture, sometimes associated with Praetorians; and common sense and known Roman taste argue an elaborate helmet for officers.

The saluting trooper - the feather on his lance marking a despatch rider - wears a known type of cavalry helmet and conventional armour; there is sculptural evidence for the hexagonal shield with a scorpion blazon (which may hono the memory of the Emperor Tiberius, whose birth-sign it was His elaborate harness decorations are from caval tombstone evidence.

The standard-bearer - like those of the legions an auxiliaries - wears ringmail, and carries a small round *parm* shield; the lion-pelt seems to have been a privilege Praetorian standard- bearers, however. A sculpture shows th standard of III Praetorian Cohort lavishly decorated wi stylised crowns, imperial images, etc., and also bearing scorpion plaque.

Sculpture also shows Praetorians with the curved ov *scutum* bearing several blazons - including that illustratec featuring moons and stars; colours are, as always, guesswo but may have varied from cohort to cohort. Although th guardsmen wear the *paenula* cloak over their articulate plate cuirasses, we have shown them parading with cre fitted to their helmets, which certainly had fixtures for th attachment; as with the tunic, modern experts now believe that white is the most likely colour.

Finally, there is written and sculptural evidence for Rome soldiers wearing woollen socks under their sandals; an common sense argues that on winter campaign duty cloth sheepskin foot-wrappings must have been worn to preve frostbite -soldiers who could not keep up with the march we soldiers wasted.

Legionaries in combat, Second Dacian War, c.105 AD

Plate 7

In 96 AD the tyrant Domitianus was assassinated; and after the brief reign of Nerva his kinsman Trajanus ascended the throne in 98. A vigorous soldier-emperor, he was to extend the empire to its greatest extent; and on Trajan's Column, his great spiral frieze monument in Rome, he left us the single finest piece of sculptural evidence for the appearance of the Roman army at its peak of glory (though interpreting the Column has divided scholars for generations).

The emphasis was now firmly on the Danube frontier, where Domitianus's campaigns had cost many casualties including the total loss of two legions (*Legio V Alaudae* and *XXI Rapax*); the threat from Dacia, temporarily averted by treaty, was the new emperor's first concern. In 101-102 he led ten legions in an offensive which ended with agreed terms and garrisons planted in Dacian territory. In 105 the warlike King Decebalus of Dacia attacked across the Danube once more; again the emperor took the field, leading a massive army with elements of no fewer than 13 legions and similar numbers of auxiliaries - probably half Rome's total available forces. Before he won final victory and incorporated Dacia into the empire his army saw hard fighting against an enemy dangerous enough to force modifications to their equipment.

Recovered helmets and sculpted evidence from a war memorial suggest that Imperial-pattern helmets and articulated cuirasses were not proof in hand-to-hand combat against the Dacians' heavy, scythe-like *falx* swords, and that these must have been particularly deadly when delivering sweeping blows against the arms and legs. Helmets were hastily fitted with extra crossed reinforcing bars over the skull; this style long outlasted the Dacian Wars and so may have been more or less universal. At least some legionary infantry were also issued with extra limb armour resembling that used in the gladiatorial arena - articulated plates protecting the right or both arms, greaves for the left or both shins, and extra leather *pteruges*. (Some are also shown at this date wearing half-breeches under their tunics, like auxiliaries - the reason is unknown.)

Here a Dacian charge crashes into a legionary unit. In th centre a soldier stands over a comrade hacked down with terrible thigh wound, and manages to dispatch his enemy classic style - knocking him off balance with a punching blo from the upheld shield, and stabbing upwards round its edg into the tribesman's left ribs. At left, a legionary wearing an c bronze version of the Imperial Gallic helmet presses forwar his bronze-edged plywood shield badly damaged by *fc* blows; note its construction - the only recovered example h three layers of wooden strips glued in alternating directior the outer layer of leather (painted here with a blazon from th Column).

We choose to show this squad wearing mixed gear - som in the articulated "Corbridge" cuirass depicted on Trajar Column, some in shirts of small iron scales or ringmail, as shov on the Adamklissi memorial, some with curved rectangu shields, some with the curved "clipped oval" shape seen c other monuments - to dramatise the fact that historians ha no real idea how uniform Roman equipment was in any giv unit at any given time. Armour was presumably made many dispersed smiths; the modern idea of mass productic to exact patterns was alien to their culture; metal equipme lasts for years, even decades, and would never be discarde while still serviceable; we know that individual wealth a taste were allowed some play; so, given the inevitab transfers and replacements, a cohort might have presented fairly mixed appearance.

Auxiliary skirmishers, Second Dacian War, c.105 AD

Plate 8

Auxiliary infantry were recruited from non-Roman citizens, initially from the less civilised, more recently acquired provinces; they were commanded by Roman prefects (tribunes, for the units nominally 1,000 strong), and officered by centurions promoted from their ranks or from those of the legions. The basic unit was the infantry cohort; these served in campaign armies in at least equal numbers to the legionary infantry. They were not grouped into separate multi-cohort formations equivalent to legions; several cohorts were probably attached to each legion and came under its overall command. The *cohors quingenaria* comprised six centuries of 80 men each, the *cohors milliaria*, ten centuries.

Cohorts were numbered, and named for their geographic origins - at the simplest, e.g. *Cohors I Noricorum*, the 1st Cohort raised from the people of Noricum, roughly modern Austria. Others also bore the name of the emperor under whom they were raised (e.g. *Ulpia*, from one of the names of Trajanus); honorific titles marking victorious service (e.g. *Victrix*), loyalty (e.g. *Pia Fidelis*), block award of Roman citizenship for distinguished service (*civium Romanorum*), etc. By Trajanus's reign there were about 132 *quingenariae* and 18 *milliariae* cohorts of auxiliary infantry in service.

It is usually suggested that most auxiliary foot wore ringmail armour, helmets (often bronze) broadly similar to but simpler than the legionary type, and half-breeches under the tunic. Normal swords were carried; but instead of the heavy line-of-battle legionary's *pila* javelins and large curved *scutum* shield, a simpler all-purpose spear (*hasta*) and a smaller oval shield (see Plate 10).

After serious mutinies in the 1st century AD auxiliaries were generally posted far from their home province for many years, later recruiting locally around their stations; in many cases their particular nationality thus probably survived only in their titles. An exception seems to have been the policy of employing some units retaining traditional regional weapons (e.g. Cretan archers, slingers from the Balearic Isles); tombstones of men from cohorts of e.g. Syrian archers suggest

that these units with special skills were kept up to strength wit[h] drafts from home.

Always exposed in the van, rear and on the flanks of fie[ld] armies, auxiliaries were used for scouting, skirmishing an[d] screening. These three types are shown on Trajan's Colum[n.] The archer with a segmented helmet, mailshirt, long gow[n] and powerful Eastern composite bow, is probably from th[e] Sarmatian Iazyges people of the Black Sea coast. (Othe[r] archers are shown in absolutely conventional auxilia[ry] costume.) One skirmisher (right) wears a wolf-pelt over h[is] helmet - in early Roman times, the mark of light javelin troop[s] - and carries a shield with this blazon. Another auxilia[ry] (background) has this legionary shield, and perhaps serves [in] one of the confusingly named *cohortes scutatae*. (Mode[rn] experts question the clear distinction traditionally mad[e] between legionary and auxiliary armour and weapons, citi[ng] tombstone sculptures which certainly break all the "rules" [of] identification.)

The dead legionary is taken from a carving at Mainz; b[y] elimination, his shield blazon may be that of *Legio I Adiutr[ix,]* originally raised from naval personnel. One interpretation al[so] shows the "eyebrows" embossed on the carved figure[s'] Gallic helmet extended into a fish shape. We follow this, an[d] - quite arbitrarily - give the legionary's kit some elements [of] blue, the colour associated with Roman sailors; this is pu[re] invention on our part.

18

Centurion and legionaries in camp, c.115 AD

Plate 9

One of the Romans' great tactical strengths was their marching discipline. They constructed an entrenched, pallisaded camp even for a one-night bivouac; the camp was of the same basic design whether for a single cohort or a legion, so trained soldiers could pitch it quickly by a practised routine, and could find their way around it even in the dark. Surveyors went ahead to select the site and lay out its main lines with flags and pegs. The men marched directly to the place selected for their century's tent street - ten eight-man tents of goat leather, with a larger tent for the centurion at the end, and prescribed areas for their baggage mules and gear. Part stood guard while others stacked their kit, threw up an earth and turf rampart with spoil from an outer ditch, pallisaded it with double-ended wooden stakes, and pitched the tents.

Here two legionaries, serving under Trajanus in Armenia during his last great campaign against the Parthians, help each other take off their armour - the articulated cuirass came off like a jacket once the front thongs and buckles were unfastened; and note the felt-lined helmet at their feet. Their comrade, stripped to his tunic but always wearing his dagger belt (the belt, and the consequent hitching up of the tunic above the knees, was the proud mark of the soldier) prepares the evening meal; the basic campaign ration was grain, cooked into a porridge or baked into rough loaves by the campfire, but vegetables and meat would be added where they could be gathered or bought locally.

The duty centurion exercising his humour on the cook wears dazzling full-dress uniform, and gallantry decorations (*phalerae*) displayed on a harness over the silvered scale armour appropriate to his wealth. The graded career structure of the professional junior officers was another "modern" feature of the army, up to that time unique in the world, and an important foundation of Rome's military prowess. Each of the legion's 59 centuries (including the five double-size centuries of the elite First Cohort) was commanded by a centurion, usually a ranker promoted

through the "NCO" grades, but sometimes a "direct entry" officer through family influence - even Roman equestrian, the lower class of propertied gentry, sometimes chose th career path for its good prospects rather than trying to secur a post as an auxiliary unit commander. It was no job for weak or squeamish man - centurions enforced their authorit freely with blows of their vinesticks, and routinely exacte bribes to let soldiers off fatigues; but they were th professional backbone of the empire, long-service veteran who led the troops in battle by personal example. Their ran has no modern equivalent but, roughly, they filled the post held today by all ranks from senior sergeants up to lieutenan colonels, moving up through the numbered cohorts of legion by promotion into vacancies. Above the senio centurion of the First Cohort (*primipilus*, "first spear") the 5,50 man legion had only a handful of staff tribunes, most of ther with between four and eight years' service, and th commanding officer (*legatus*) himself.

Centurions' pay was generous, starting at five times soldier's annual rate (1,500 silver *denarii*, compared to 300) the *primi ordines*, centurions of the First Cohort, drew ten time a soldier's pay, and the "first spear" 20 times. If they lived collect, their discharge bonuses could be huge: und Caligula (c.40 AD) that of a *primipilus* was 150,000 *dena* equal to hundreds of years' pay for a legionary - but at an time there were only about 30 of these supreme experienced soldiers serving with the legions. Centurions ofte transferred between legions; many desirable staff jobs we open to senior grades, as were major civil service posts aft retirement, which could lift a whole family into the monie ruling classes.

Auxiliaries of a Cohors Equitata in action, Northern Britain, c.118 AD

Plate 10

Offensive operations in Britain ended with Julius Agricola's victory in 84 AD in north-east Scotland; but with the withdrawal of troops for Domitianus's Danube campaigns plans to occupy Scotland (Caledonia) were abandoned, and a chain of forts across the country roughly from modern Carlisle to Newcastle marked - in Roman minds - their border. It was often disturbed, by both attacks from the north and risings to the south; and there was a serious outbreak in 117-118.

In such operations much of the fighting was normally done by auxiliary units; even in pitched battles the legionaries were often held back as a reserve. Indeed, we read of one hard-fought victory achieved "without Roman casualties" - meaning that the auxiliaries did all the fighting and paid the whole butcher's bill.

Apart from the cavalry *ala* and the infantry *cohors* (see Plates 5 and 8) there was a third type of auxiliary unit, also listed in two sizes, roughly 600 or roughly 1,000 strong: the mixed *cohors equitata*. At least 130 of the total of some 280 auxiliary cohorts were of this type - usefully versatile for warfare in all kinds of terrain and, with their longer "reach", for patrolling from frontier outposts. The *cohors equitata quingenaria* probably had six 80-man centuries of foot and four 32-man *turmae* (cavalry troops); and the *milliaria* equivalent, ten centuries and eight troops.

In battle the foot and horse components probably fought separately, the infantry and cavalry of several units being brigaded together for tactical purposes. The troopers of mixed cohorts were paid less than those of the *alae*; there is evidence that while their horses and gear were of lower quality, they had the same weapons and fought according to the same drills. Basic weapons were the dual-purpose spear and light javelins; and while there were some specifically named archer units, it seems that at least some men in all units were trained with the bow.

Among the auxiliaries shown on Trajan's Column, wearing the usual ringmail, and short breeches beneath their tunics,

are one trooper and one foot soldier carrying shields with th[e] same blazon, but that of the trooper with an extra "spine" perhaps a strengthening bar; we show the blazon here in us[e] by a mixed cohort. The infantry, armed with the auxiliary *hasta* fighting spear rather than the legionary's *pilum*, catc[h] their breath after successfully driving their Celtic enemies o[ff] the crest of a slope; the troopers - note the *turma* standard ride pass their flank to exploit forwards. All wear bron[ze] helmets, simpler than the legionary type; examples with th[e] "post-Dacian" crossed reinforcement have been foun[d]. Auxiliaries' tombstones show standard legionary-style swor[ds] and dagger-belts with aprons.

We copy the design of the century's standard (and th[e] bearer's wolf-pelt with the mask cut off, perhaps peculiar [to] auxiliaries?) from one of an Asturian cohort from norther[n] Spain. Another such unit - *Cohors II Asturum Equitat[a]* honoured for loyal service in Domitianus's reign with th[e] additional title *Pia Fidelis Domitiana* - served in Britain aroun[d] this period. One reference suggests that men in that regio[n] traditionally wore black; without evidence, we have chose[n] to show them wearing that colour (though it seems unlike[ly] that regional distinctions would survive long service abroa[d]).

The centurion might be a promoted former legionary whose next step up, if he is lucky and successful, will be to [a] centurion's post in a legion. We show our officer [in] conventional, if rather plain centurion's costume; no speci[fic] differences for auxiliary centurions are known.

Legionaries building a frontier fort, c.120 AD

Plate 11

In 117 Trajanus was succeeded by his nephew and former staff officer Hadrianus; as energetic as his predecessor, he concentrated not on expansion but on consolidation. He travelled tirelessly around the imperial frontiers, supervising the construction of lines of strategic defence. Rome had always built frontier forts between campaigns; now they appeared in mutually supporting chains along borders which were intended to be permanent. On the border of Britannia and Caledonia he even built the unique, 70-mile continuous stone wall which today bears his name. Though Rome launched many further offensives, Hadrianus's reign marks an ominous change towards a basically defensive posture, under steadily growing pressures.

Most public works in frontier provinces were carried out by the legions themselves. They built the roads they marched on, and the forts they garrisoned. The ranks included many skilled specialists of all kinds, from clerks and surveyors to smiths and masons; and although such soldiers did not all earn extra pay they enjoyed the status of *immunes* - men excused routine fatigues.

Fort ramparts were initially made of earth dug from an outer defensive ditch, piled on a rubble or timber foundation, and walled front and rear with piled turfs; they stood about ten feet high, with a timber parapet protecting a broad wall-walk adding about another six feet. Gatehouses and corner and interval watchtowers were of timber. (By Trajanus's reign some older forts were already being rebuilt with stone-faced ramparts.) Inside were barracks, stores, headquarters, etc. for (usually) a single cohort, either *quingenaria* or *milliaria*. Fort design is discussed in more detail elsewhere in this book.

Here, Hadrianic legionaries have almost finished the main defences of a cohort fort in the hills of the military zone of northern Britain - which was seldom peaceful for long, given the links between tribes such as the Selgovae and Novantae in free Caledonia, and the irreconcilable Brigantes of the occupied zone. It is significant that such a small province had a garrison of three legions (*Legio II Augusta* at Caerleon in south Wales; *XX Valeria Victrix* at Chester in the weste midlands; and *IX Hispana*, later *VI Victrix*, at York controllin the north-east), as well as about 20 auxiliary cavalry and 5 infantry units scattered all over the north and west.

There is good evidence for Roman building methods an tools. Cranes were braced with cables and powered b treadmills; baskets were used for carrying earth and rubb saw-pits, much like those used until a hundred years ag were set up on site to produce planks; clay and straw we puddled to make daub for wattle building panels.

Note the soldiers' tunics, with a wide slit at the neck; th was reduced for everyday wear by gathering a handful the slack cloth into a knot behind the neck. For hea labouring the knot was untied, and the slit was then lor enough for one arm to pass through, freeing the shoulder. Th *optio*, with his staff of rank, has tucked in his dagger belt notebook made from smooth wooden plaques linke concertina-fashion; and carries a larger wooden tablet wi an applied surface of soft wax, in which he can write with metal stylus, smoothing the wax anew to erase his jottin Although soldiers on campaign probably always neglecte shaving - Romans did not usually carry personal razors b were shaved by barbers - in the early 2nd Century sho beards became fashionable when the emperors adopte this style.

Legionaries in marching order, c.130 AD

Plate 12

The legions normally had permanent fortresses some distance inside the frontiers, the border posts being held by auxiliary units. However, from time to time legionary detachments held such forts, sometimes sharing the larger posts with auxiliary cohorts or *alae*. This could occur during long periods of active operations, when the legionaries wintered on the frontier.

"Vexillations" of a thousand men or more were often transferred from the legions' permanent bases in time of need: to reinforce a nearby frontier, to be temporarily shipped overseas to take part in a faraway campaign, or simply to help in some major engineering project. Because all 30-odd legions were spread between the provinces it was difficult to reinforce one sector in an emergency without dangerously weakening another, so assembling *ad hoc* "task forces" from vexillations was more common than transferring whole legions - though this, too, was done during major wars. Britain's garrison was weakened by large vexillations for the civil war of 69 AD and for the Chatti war in 84; detachments from Germany came to replace the casualties of the Boudiccan war in 61, and from Spain and Germany to help stabilise the northern frontier and build Hadrian's Wall in c.118-122. As the 2nd Century progressed units were moved steadily from the Rhine to the Danube frontier.

The great network of stone-flagged roads built by the legions all over the empire were superb strategic arteries, and legionaries - hardened by three route-marches a month even in peacetime - were renowned for their marching: 24 Roman miles (36km) a day, for hundreds of miles if need be. The legionary carried his gear lashed to a forked or T-shaped pole, resting low down behind his shoulders where it balanced well, and locked his slung shield in place. Sometimes, like the right hand man here, the pack was slung from his *dolabra* pickaxe instead of a pole; on the march the blade edge was covered with a bronze guard. Helmets were slung from the shoulder armour.

The basic marching kit included a cross-braced leather satchel for personal effects, a bronze messtin (*patera*) an cooking pot, canvas or leather bags for spare clothing an grain rations, and probably a waterskin in a net bag. Sinc armour and weapons weighed some 45lbs.(20kg), the tota load must have approached 65lbs.(30kg).

The legionary's standard foul-weather cloak (*paenula*) c thick yellow-brown wool was hooded, and fastened on th centre of the chest with buttons or toggles. Cavalry an officers wore a simpler rectangular cloak (*sagum*) brooche at the right shoulder.

Outside the fort was usually found a levelled parad ground, and a communal bathhouse (regarded by c Romans as a basic necessity, and used as a social club); an archaeology has also revealed quite large and well-bu villages. Apart from inns for official travellers, such village would doubtless offer shadier drinking-dens to serve th needs of the rank and file, craftsmen's workshops, smithie trader's shops and booths, and quarters for the soldier unofficial families.

Roman soldiers - legionary and auxiliary - were forbidde to marry during their service, but the authorities turned a blin eye to their private arrangements with local women; soldier sons were retrospectively declared legitimate on their father retirement and official marriage, and were encouraged t enlist in their turn. Here a pair of legionaries say their farewe in the village outside a stone-built fort in a frontier zone perhaps they are going to man a small local police/custom post down the road: in peacetime soldiers performed mar detached quasi-military duties.

Legionary and cavalryman on campaign, 150s AD

Plate 13

Antoninus Pius occupied the throne from 138 to 161 in relative peace, apart from a major rising in North Africa and lesser ones in Egypt and Dacia. The only major operations were in Britain.

From c.140 Hadrian's Wall was virtually abandoned; its garrisons, and those in the Pennine Hills south of it, were stripped for an offensive into Scotland - probably to support the friendly Votadini tribe of the eastern Lowlands against the hostile Selgovae to their west. By 142-143 the victorious army had established a new frontier on the Clyde-Forth line. It has been calculated that the newly occupied Scottish Lowlands were held by some 13,000 men; the turf and timber "Antonine Wall" by about 6,200; and advanced screening forts north of it, by some 4,500 - a total of around 24,000 men. The region south of Hadrian's Wall - which itself no longer presented a barrier to co-operation between the tribes - was garrisoned by only about 6,800 men. They were to prove inadequate.

In 154 the Brigantes tribe of northern England - still unreconciled to the pax Romana after some 70 years of occupation - rose in strength, far behind the active military zone, and wreaked havoc. It took about two years to defeat them, at heavy loss to the legions (the general Julius Verus had to bring reinforcements for all three British legions from the armies of both German provinces). While this war raged the Antonine Wall and the Lowlands were abandoned, and forts on Hadrian's Wall and particularly in the Pennines were repaired and reoccupied.

By 158 the Antonine frontier itself was reoccupied - only to be finally abandoned in c.163: Rome could not police the tribes of northern Britannia at the same time as holding a frontier as far north as the Clyde-Forth line. Hadrian's Wall became, once more, the edge of the Roman world.

Evidence for the legionary's appearance in the mid-2nd Century is sparser than before; it seems basically as in Trajanus's day, but perhaps simpler. The deep helmet illustrated, found in Germany, is plainer in its details. The articulated cuirass (the "Newstead" type, from finds at an important Scottish fort temporarily occupied during thes campaigns by two cohorts from Legio XX Valeria Victrix an a cavalry ala) has fewer plates and much simpler fittings.

The dagger belt is now decorated with pierced plate showing the leather in cut-out patterns; the groin apron shorter than previously; some legionaries seem to have wor half-breeches beneath their tunics, and some to have carrie the auxiliary's simple fighting spear instead of the pilum though this too was still seen. Swords with ring pommels hav been dated to this period, as have new scabbard fittings; th baldric now passed round it under a bronze bracke sometimes shaped like a dolphin - a symbol of the soul's ea passing into the Netherworld. The shield blazon illustrated - th colours of this and of the tunic are, as always, guesswork comes from sculpture of Marcus Aurelius's reign; the desig suggests a unit once formed from marines. Small iron an bronze flasks have been found on military sites in Britain an Germany; some have locking caps, suggesting that they he something more expensive than water....

The trooper wears an impressive iron and bronze helme with broad cheekguards overlapping at the chin, based o examples found in Germany and usually associated with 2n to 3rd Century cavalry. He has prick-spurs strapped over h caligae - the famous hob-nailed sandals which shod infant and cavalry alike. Auxiliaries, like legionaries, were ofte transferred in vexillations as well as in complete units, formir ad hoc regiments on campaign; many reinforcements we shipped to Britain during the wars of the 140s-160s. If shie blazons did vary from unit to unit, then these tempora regiments must have presented a motley appearance. C Trajanus's Parthian war of 115 a cavalry "task force" recorded which was formed from troopers of no less than fi different alae and fourteen cohortes equitatae.)

Barrack room in auxiliary fort, c.190 AD

Plate 14

The reign of the philosopher-emperor Marcus Aurelius (161-180) saw continuous fighting, as the first serious pressure built up against Rome's eastern frontiers. In the 160s the Chatti invaded across the Rhine, and the Parthians swept into Cappadocia and Syria. After prolonged campaigns these threats were turned back, but only by stripping the Danube garrisons; and soldiers returning from the East brought with them an epidemic plague which further weakened armies already suffering from shortage of manpower.

Between 169 and 175 the tribes across the Danube - the Marcomanni, Quadi, Sarmatii and others, themselves beginning to feel pressure from population movements far to their north-east - launched several major waves of attack. These wars saw Pannonia, Noricum and Raetia temporarily overrun, and some tribesmen actually crossed the Alps into northern Italy for a time. Marcus Aurelius's long campaigns won Rome a brief respite, enjoyed by his tyrannical son Commodus after he died, exhausted, in 180 AD.

Here troopers of an auxiliary frontier garrison relax after the day's duty. The barrack blocks in forts echoed the layout of tent lines in camp. Infantry barracks were partitioned to accomodate the century's ten eight-man squads, with their centurion's larger quarters at the end. Cavalry troops, half the size of infantry centuries, were probably housed two to a block; some barracks have an officer's quarters at each end, supporting this theory; and some blocks incorporate barrack rooms down one side and stables down the other.

Each squad had a pair of rooms: in the front room, opening onto a verandah, they kept their gear, the back room being the sleeping quarters. Typically these seem to have been about 18ft. by 12ft.; there is evidence for bunks, and a hearth for a fire or brazier. The plastered walls were of wattle and daub, the floor of concrete, the hearth probably cowled with a clay-and-rubble chimney breast, the roof tiled; there were small, high windows, sometimes glazed.

Archaeologists have not identified any central mess halls in forts; the squads may have eaten in their quarters - and cooked at least some of their rations there, too, althoug large ovens, presumably for bread, have been found dug in the inner earth slope of fort ramparts. When in garrison th enjoyed a varied diet - there is evidence for many kinds meat both farmed and game, fish, shellfish, vegetables, fru nuts, pickles and sauces; and for men buying private supplie including better wine than the army issue.

Their replacements being recruited locally or drafted from various provinces, some auxiliary units must have be fairly multi-national, though presumably using basic Latin their *lingua franca*. Off-duty, at least, they probably wore mixture of the common white wool tunic and various person garments of regional weaves. The soldier tending the hea (who keeps his money in a bronze arm-purse) wears a tunic a kind of basic tartan: clothing recovered from no European peat bogs, sometimes pre-dating Christ, is of god quality and often shows woven checkered or herringbo patterns. His belt has a ring-and-stud fastening, becomi popular at the end of the 2nd Century.

Behind him, playing a board game, a soldier wears tunic with two darker vertical stripes; this was a pattern se among civilians throughout the Roman world and ov several centuries, but we have no evidence one way or t other for its use on army tunics before the late 3rd Centu Among the pottery cups and utensils on the table lies folding claspknife.

Watching from his bunk at the right - the furthest from t draught of the door beyond the hearth, and so probably t prerogative of the squad's toughest veteran! - a scarr trooper cleans a handsome *spatha* with a polished bone and a gilt figure of a war-god inlaid into the blade. There sculptural evidence for his woollen socks without toes or hee worn under the sandals.

30

Cavalry on the Upper German frontier, c.230 AD

Plate 15

Commodus was assassinated in 192; for five years contenders put up by the Praetorian Guard and different frontier armies fought for the throne, until Septimius Severus emerged victorious. In 209, after a successful campaign against Parthia, he sailed for Britain; many troops had been withdrawn during the civil war, and Caledonian tribesmen had poured over the northern frontier. Severus and his son Caracalla drove them back and mounted major campaigns deep inside Scotland; but when Severus died at York in 210 Caracalla concluded a treaty and withdrew the army to strengthened positions along Hadrian's Wall. Britain - almost alone of the provinces - would have relative peace for many years.

Caracalla campaigned successfully on the Rhine and Danube frontiers, which were under pressure from a new tribal confederation, the Alamanni; but during operations against Parthia in 217 he too was assassinated. Now began 60 years of anarchy which fatally weakened the armies and ruined the economy, as an endless series of pretenders stripped the frontier garrisons, their brief reigns convulsed by endemic civil wars, mutinies, and constant barbarian invasions.

The German frontier was not defended by a continuous wall, as in Britain, but marked by a pallisade and ditch studded with watchtowers, and guarded by a chain of the usual cohort forts. Here, on a winter morning during the reign of Severus Alexander, a patrol from a cavalry unit arrive too late at the site of a breakthrough by a war party of Alamanni tribesmen.

Since 212, in the face of constant manpower shortages, the distinction between legionary and auxiliary recruiting had disappeared: henceforth all free-born men within the empire were granted citizenship, and were eligible for the legions. At the turn of the century marked changes in military costume, too, began to be seen in tombstone and other sculpture.

Most tunics now had long sleeves; and long Teutonic-style trousers were worn by legionary and auxiliary alike. The classic openwork *caliga* sandal seems to have been replaced by more solid shoes and boots, though still with cut-out lace panels on the vamp. The hooded infantry *paenula* clo began to give way, for all troops, to the cavalry's simp rectangular *sagum*, often fringed, and pinned on the rig shoulder with various brooches - the "crossbow" shape w common. The infantry also copied the cavalry in beginning use longer *spatha* swords, slung now on the left, from broc baldrics with large cut-out decorative plates and terminals disc-shaped scabbard chapes are characteristic of Germ finds.

Here a decurion is being shown the axe of a wounde and abandoned raider, who has just been dispatched aft questioning by a local scout from an irregular tribal ur (*cuneus* or *numerus*) of the sort now increasingly attached the overstretched frontier garrisons. The officer wears bronze scale cuirass fastening by means of decorated che plates; its semi-rigid construction limits its length to the wa for ease of hip movement, and heavy leather *pterug* protect his arms and pelvis.

His heavily embossed tinned bronze helmet of "Atti shape is copied from a recovered example from Germany. bears scratched owner's details: in fact, despite its appare richness, it belonged to a common trooper, and from a lov *cohors equitata* at that: Aliquandus, in the *turma* of Decuri Nonus, of the Spanish *cohors I Bracaraugustanorum*...). V have therefore given his trumpeter another of several similc elaborate examples found. For lack of any later evidence v show a cavalry shield blazon from Trajan's Column.

Doctor treating cavalry officer, early 3rd Century AD

Plate 16

The 3rd Century is a notorious gap in the archaeological and sculptural record of Roman military equipment. We have a few finds - helmets, weapons and scraps of armour, very few of them closely datable; a few weathered tombstones (which typically show "undress" uniform rather than armour); and a few tiny, crude images on commemorative coins. Interpretation must always be little more than educated guesswork.

During the years 217-284 AD the empire sank into chaos - some 40 men were proclaimed as emperor, at least locally, many of them simultaneous rivals; of these only one died a natural death (of plague - which again swept across the empire from the East, causing famine and depopulation in some regions). Military manpower, deployments, and logistics were all ruinously affected - not least by hyper-inflation, which reduced the value of the silver currency by a factor of a hundred, further crippling state administration. While opposing generals struggled for imperial power, the Parthians attacked in the East; the Goths in the Balkans; the Marcomanni, Quadi and Sarmatians over the Danube; the Alamanni into Upper Germany, Raetia and northern Italy; the Franks into Lower Germany and Gaul, even reaching Spain.

Here, in his quarters in a frontier fort, a cavalry officer lies mortally wounded by a javelin which has struck up under his waist-length scale cuirass. This lies discarded, with his handsome iron and bronze helmet; note the pointed browguard, and the plume - later writings associate yellow with the cavalry.

The classic officer career, for a man of "equestrian" social rank in Rome's clearly defined class structure, started with a commission as prefect of an auxiliary cohort. After three or four years in post men of proven competence hoped for appointment as one of the half-dozen tribunes on the staff of a legion. Even fewer reached the third step - command of a cavalry *ala*; and a few of the best might hope to take over one of the larger *milliaria* cavalry regiments.

Medical officers and orderlies were attached to Roman units in the field, and hospitals have been tentative identified at some forts; known names suggest that som doctors were Greeks. (The Romans held Greece in speci regard as the cradle of civilisation, and it was the on province not obliged to provide auxiliary cohorts for th army.) Well-made surgical instruments for many specialise uses have been found; many herbal remedies were know but wounds like this - inevitably involving chronic shock, bloc loss, internal injury and infection - would normally have bee beyond the doctor's powers.

An infantry comrade tries to comfort the wounded ma His enormously deep bronze helmet is the last known examp showing unbroken development from the classic "Imperic legionary style. Ringmail and scale armour had probab replaced the articulated cuirass entirely before the middle the century; the latest sculptured example dates from c.20 and the latest datable fragments are from a site in use c.22 260 AD. His *spatha* hangs from a characteristic broad baldr its pierced bronze plates sometimes bore a good-luck mot (e.g. "Jupiter Greatest and Best, Protect This Unit, Soldiers All"

Officers' quarters in forts were plastered and painted lil civilian homes. This officer keeps a slave/mistress, who hol an oil lamp for the doctor; such relationships were sometime long and affectionate, but quite distinct from the form obligations of marriage between families of the equestric class.

Legionaries in battle against Parthian/Sassanian horse-archers Mesopotamia, c.260 AD

Plate 17

From the 1st Century BC onwards the Scythian kings of Parthia (roughly modern Iraq and Iran) were Rome's most persistent rivals. The two empires were too rich, too avaricious, and too nearly contiguous to co-exist in peace; and each was too strong, with too great a strategic depth, to ever suffer final and decisive defeat. In virtually every reign Roman armies campaigned against Parthia, either in the buffer-state of Armenia or in Mesopotamia itself. Sometimes (as under Nero's great general Corbulo, and Trajanus) they won notable victories and installed garrisons beyond the Euphrates; sometimes they suffered shattering defeats; most often, they were led deep into the wilderness by elusive cavalry armies, only to withdraw in frustration.

In 226 AD the Parthian monarchy was overthrown, and the kingdom incorporated into a greater empire, by the Sassanian Persians from the south. The Sassanids profited from Roman disunity; and in 260 their King Shapur inflicted a catastrophic defeat at Edessa on the Emperor Valerian, killing him and taking tens of thousands of legionaries into slavery. This war left historians the priceless gift of Dura Europos, a captured Roman fortress on the Euphrates where helmets, armour, shields and wall-paintings survived amazingly intact.

Here a legionary stands over a fallen officer, while javelineers fight off horse-archers deceived by the dust-clouds into venturing too close. In the absence of firm evidence our reconstructions are tentative, but logical. The previous identification of the often-found helmet at left as a cavalry type is challenged today; it seems equally likely to be heavy infantry issue, and several similar finds have been made on sites associated with infantry (including legionary) units. Its notable features are the pointed, up-tilted browguard, and huge cheekguards covering the ears (once thought to be solely a cavalry feature) and overlapping in front of the chin.

Ringmail shirts with short, half-length, and long sleeves all appear among the evidence; some have been found with decorative bronze mail strips incorporated. Dished oval shields have been found, painted pink; an early copy of wall-painting shows various other pale colours, and the typ of blazons illustrated - crude foliate wreaths and sprays i black or white. This legionary fights defensively with his *pilum* (now a socketed rather than tanged type); since the 2n Century at least, the legions occasionally fought again dangerous enemy cavalry by forming a tight phalanx sever ranks deep, the rear ranks throwing their *pila* over the head of this wall of braced shields and spears.

Wall-paintings show purple edging to officers' whit tunics. Complete shirts of bronze ringmail are known; here w guess at the fastening chest-plates, as also associated wit scale cuirasses. His decorated iron and bronze helmet has plume knob, an up-tilted pointed browguard, a pointed edg above the nose, and cheekguards meeting over the chi The inside of his flat oval shield, copied from a superb Dur Europos find, is highly decorated; the outside was red, wit complex multi-coloured friezes and an astonishing Amazo battle scene.

There is sculptural and written evidence that from th early 3rd Century different men within the legion we equipped with several different types of fighting spear an throwing javelin; a legionary of *Legio II Parthica*, raised k Septimius Severus, is shown with a bundle of five javelins, an we reconstruct a slung quiver as logical (though the on direct reference to javelin quivers applies to cavalrymen). Th javelineers' helmets have the crossed reinforces or embossed rather than attached; they are taken from datable contemporary German find.

Cavalry officer, c.306 AD

Plate 18

In the 260s-280s a series of tough soldier-emperors from Illyricum (roughly modern Yugoslavia) managed to partly restore the frontiers by incessant campaigning. Diocletianus (r.284-305), an administrative genius, built on the improvisations of his predecessors to organise a military system wholly different from the old army - a system further developed by Constantinus (r.306-337). Diocletianus divided responsibility between two co-emperors, for the East and West, each with a picked deputy (to whom, in theory, he would eventually hand over power). Constantinus, who ruled alone, moved his capital from Rome to Constantinople (Istanbul).

The army was divided between static frontier troops (*limitanei*), and much stronger mobile field armies, which the defence of the empire now demanded. Vexillations from the old frontier legions and auxiliaries, and new units, formed regional field armies called *comitatenses*, and the emperors' central reserve units or *palatini*. Field army units still included "legions", but now only some 1,000 strong; a few, formed from detachments of the old frontier legions, kept their traditional titles (e.g. *Legio V Macedonica*), but others had new-style names (e.g. the newly raised *Ioviani* and *Herculiani*). Cavalry units were assembled from every possible source, old and new, and were increasingly important.

The long civil wars, barbarian invasions, collapse of the economy, plague, famine, and loss of territory all contributed to a chronic shortage of men and money; Diocletianus made military service by soldiers' sons compulsory, and the army was now paid not in cash but in food, clothing and other materials, with occasional bounties in un- debased gold coinage. Apart from these conscripts, from this period on increasing numbers of "Roman" soldiers would be German or Gothic mercenaries, often serving in well equipped 500-strong *auxilia palatini* - both barbarians from beyond the frontiers, and settlers whose incursions were regularised by treaty. Their chieftain/ officers could rise to the highest ranks in Roman service.

The army's appearance was as different as its characte as we see in this plate. In an old military graveyard beside Roman road, an officer broods over the aftermath of a batt during the brief civil war which established Constantinus rule. Sculpture, mosaics and surviving metal objects suggest costume influenced by Rome's eastern and Danubian allie and enemies.

Long-sleeved tunics now bear edge-stripes and appliqu patches on skirt and shoulder, often in purple or maroo number and shape may indicate rank or some other kind o status. Trousers often resemble medieval footed hose, tight t the leg and passing inside the shoe. Germanic-style belts wide, with bronze plates and stiffeners, and narrowe secondary straps supporting the scabbard - replace baldric

The supply of equipment seems to have been bac disrupted during the civil wars. Scale and ringmail shirts are s worn; but the long line of "Imperial" helmets has ende Instead of their deep, skilfully-worked single-piece skulls w find simpler types, of separate segments rivetted to framework sometimes with a nasal bar, and cheek- ar neckguards sewn or strapped to the leather lining. The soldi lying dead beneath a *manuballista* (a man-portable arro shooting catapult) wears a crude, cheap example; th officer has a very elaborate gilt version, with large pas "jewels", and a crest raised on thick rivets. Although a co shows Constantinus wearing such a helmet some similar fin - as before - bear owners' marks suggesting that even th most elaborate did not always belong to officers; they m perhaps have identified high-status palatine cavalry?

In the background ride troopers of one of the units arme (since Hadrianus's reign) with the *contus*, a lance abo 12ft.long, which was used two-handed; it was probak copied from the Sarmatians, like the *draco* standard. This ho a metal animal head and a multi-coloured fabric "windsoc body; it was in use by Roman cavalry during the 2nd Centu and by the legions from c.260 AD.

Catapult in action on the Saxon Shore, c.340 AD

Plate 19

The 3rd-4th Century reforms included a huge programme of fortification. Since the frontier garrisons, thinned out by the manpower demands of the field armies, were now little more than "trip- wires" to buy time in the face of invasions which had become incessant due to massive population movements beyond the north-east frontiers, the towns and military depots in the interior needed defensive walls. One specific chain of new and rebuilt defences were the large stone forts along the Saxon Shore - the eastern and southern coasts of Britain, facing the growing scourge of seaborne Germanic raiders from c.270 onwards. These often defended naval bases, typically to guard estuaries from infiltration; from their harbours blue-sailed ships with blue-clad crews patrolled the threatened coasts.

The garrison of Britain had been stripped of troops so often (as it would be again) to fight civil wars or to resist continental invasions that its strength is uncertain. The titles of old legionary and auxiliary units are still found among the *limitanei* holding Hadrian's Wall against the northern tribes (now termed the Picts), and the coastal forts against raiders from both free Germany and, later, Ireland. The *limitanei* were strung out in weak units - anything from a hundred to a few hundred men - permanently based at frontier forts, surrounded by their villages, families and fields. They have been compared to a hereditary rural militia, but this is probably exaggerated: they were sometimes transferred wholesale to field armies, so must still have been militarily significant.

Trouble on the northern frontier in c.342 brought the Emperor Constans with part of his field army to Britain; he also strengthened the Saxon Shore defences and appointed a regional commander over them. Further rumblings in the north, coastal raids, civil wars and troop withdrawals were followed, in 367, by disaster; massive and apparently co-ordinated raids by the Picts from Scotland, the Attacotti from Ireland, and Franks and Saxons from the continent overran the garrison and devastated Britain for two years before the

general Theodosius restored order with field army units.

This officer (left) and his men wear the type of uniform common in contemporary mosaics. The troops wear "ridge helmets", so called from excavated examples cheaply made in two halves, the central join covered by a ridged centre strip; these were probably mass-produced in the new government factories set up by Diocletianus to service the regional armies. The officer's is a handsomely silvered and gilt variation on the same basic construction. Sewn-on tunic strips and patches were of various shapes, numbers and colours; later garments surviving from Roman Egypt suggest that some had complex patterns in fine embroidery. The broad Germanic belts have many bronze fittings, including characteristic "propellor"-shaped stiffeners. The oval shield (background) bears a blazon identified in a half-understood early 5th Century document as that of the *Secunda Britannica*, a small regional field army unit perhaps formed from the British garrison's old *Legio II Augusta*.

The heavy catapult called an *onager* ("wild ass", from its massive kick) is reconstructed here after a written description and modern experiments. It was simpler to make than the sophisticated light field catapults (see Plate 4), though used only in positional fighting. Traversing by means of manpower and levers must have been difficult, but contemporary battle descriptions make clear that it was feasible. In modern experiments a reconstructed two-ton *onager* threw 3.62kg (8lb.) stone balls nearly 460m (500 yards); there are also ancient descriptions of pitch-soaked incendiary ammunition, and common sense suggests that this could be useful against enemy ships.

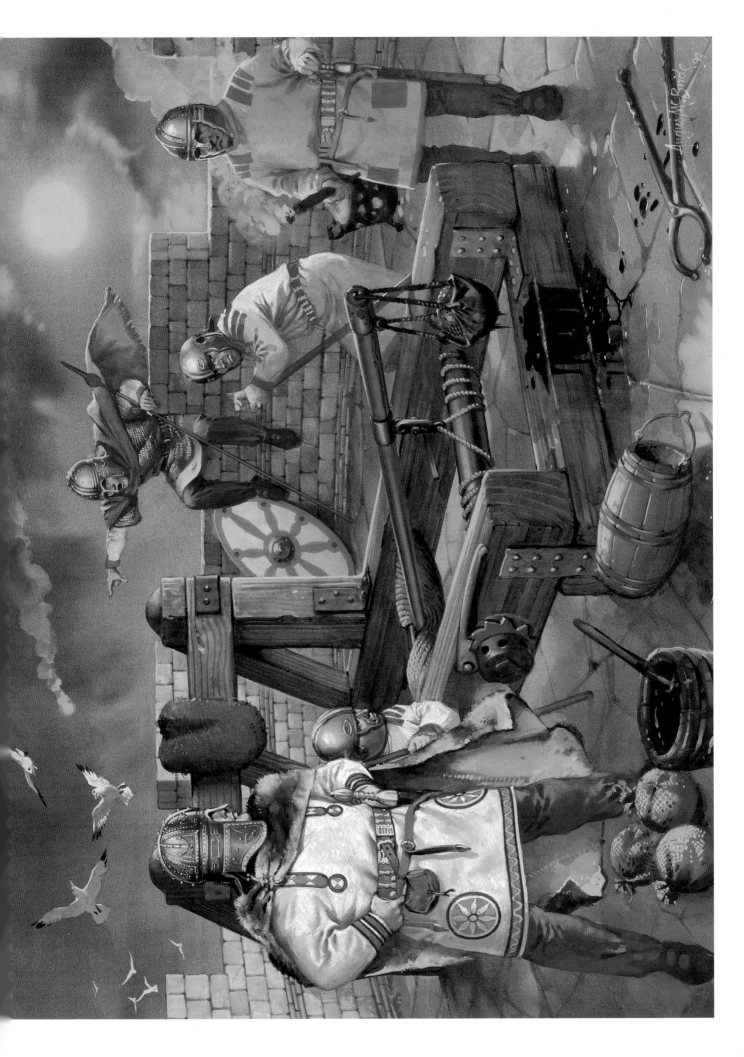

The battle of Hadrianopolis, 378 AD

Plate 20

In 376 AD the Visigoths, pressed against the Danube frontier by the advancing Huns, received permission from Valens, Roman Emperor of the East, to settle inside the empire on condition that they were disarmed. Some 200,000 starving people - a whole migrating nation - crossed the river; but maltreatment by Roman officials soon provoked them onto the war trail once more.

In summer 378 Valens led some 60,000 men of the eastern army from Constantinople north-west into Thrace. Near Hadrianopolis (modern Edirne) he waited to be joined by his teenaged nephew Gratian, Emperor of the West; but an unexpected encounter with Fritigern's Visigoth army prompted him to advance before these reinforcements arrived. On the stiflingly hot afternoon of 9 August 378 the Roman army attacked the huge Gothic wagon-circle. The Roman infantry were locked in combat when the Gothic and allied Alan cavalry charged on both wings, driving the flanking Roman cavalry from the field. The Gothic infantry swept round the Roman flanks and rear, surrounding them in a compacted mass. Parched, confused, blinded by dust, flinching under a hail of arrows, the Roman army was butchered: Valens died, and two-thirds of his men were killed or captured. Rome never recovered from this disaster; and for the few years left to her, her armies largely comprised Gothic, Alan, and even Hun mercenaries.

This desperate knot of legionaries, auxiliaries and troopers of Valens's doomed army, surrounded but making as good an ending as they can, bear little resemblance to the classic legionaries illustrated on Plate 3. But why should they, when as wide a gulf of time separates them as that between Marlborough's redcoats and today's paratroopers? Their government has been settled for fifty years in a Greek city in Asia Minor; their costume and gear have long been influenced by enemies and allies from beyond the Danube.

Most wear ridge-helmets of strikingly similar, and thus presumably mass-produced types found in Hungary and Germany; stitch-holes suggest that the leather lining was turned outside the edges. Their tunics bear characteristi[c] appliqué embroidered patches, stripes and caping; shiel[d] blazons are largely based on those shown for palatine units o[f] the Eastern emperor's field army in the early 5th Centu[ry] *Notitia Dignitatum*, a partly understood document surviving [in] two conflicting copies.

At far left a soldier displays the wheel-shaped blazon liste[d] for the *Lanciarii Seniores*, the army's senior *legio palatin[a]*. Next to him the red oval shield marks the *Bucinobantes*, a[n] *auxilium palatinum* raised from Germans allowed to settle [in] Britain. Modern experiments suggest that the lead-weighte[d] *martiobarbulus* dart, of which five were carried fixed behin[d] the shield in some way, was thrown underarm to plunge dow[n] behind enemy shields; one is poised here by a soldier of th[e] *Martiarii Seniores*, a *legio palatina*.

In the centre, one standing defiant over the other[']s corpse, are two men of elite guard cavalry units - *scolae*; the[ir] handsome helmets are based on finds at Budapest, Hunga[ry] and Concesti, Romania; and note that wrist-length ringma[il] shirts are shown in several sculpted and painted sources. A[t] the right, a junior officer holds the *draco* standard of his un[it;] his metal - crested helmet is taken from one found at Intercis[a,] Hungary, and a catacomb wall painting in Syracuse, Sicil[y.] (Some sources suggest that such helmets also existed wi[th] similar crests of stiff hair.) The Syracuse painting also shows th[e] (most unusually, red) tunic, with purple *clavi*; and a shie[ld] resembling that held over him by the soldier at far right. Th[is] kind of blazon with paired, opposed animal heads from [a] single "neck" occurs several times in the *Notitia*, sometimes f[or] light infantry *auxilia palatina*, one of them a unit of Britons.

THE ROMAN EMPIRE

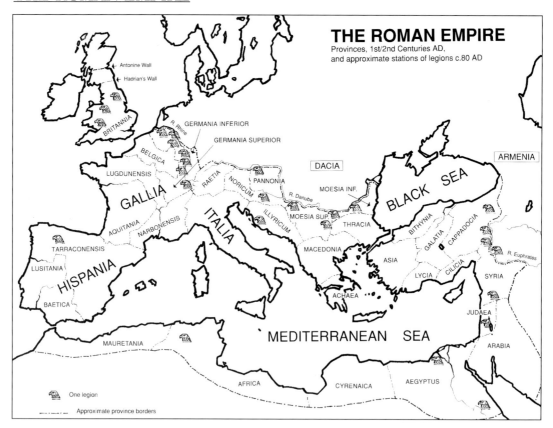

THE ROMAN EMPIRE
Provinces, 1st/2nd Centuries AD,
and approximate stations of legions c.80 AD

Rome's typical method of conquest was not outright invasion. Trade and diplomatic links were first established with a free people beyond the frontier. Subsidies were offered to selected chiefs; a protagonist in an internal quarrel was supported, helped to victory, then turned into a Roman puppet; pressure was applied to accept some form of protectorate; and only then were the legions sent in, at a time of strife, to protect Roman interests. Subsequent rebellions were put down with genocidal ferocity, while the ruling class was bribed and flattered to accept the very real material advantages of Roman rule.

The empire inherited by Augustus in c.30 BC would not be very greatly enlarged thereafter. During his reign the Teutoburg Forest disaster halted expansion in Germany beyond a Rhineland buffer zone. Claudius and Nero added England and Wales; Trajanus expanded the empire to its greatest extent in c.115 AD, with Dacia and Mesopotamia annexed, but both were too vulnerable to be held permanently. From c.120 AD onwards the frontiers ceased to be jumping-off lines for further expansion, and became a hugely long defensive perimeter. Its defenders were spread far too thinly to resist indefinitely the growing pressure of external attacks - and the plague of civil war which ravaged the empire in the decades after 218 AD fatally weakened them.

The later 2nd and 3rd Centuries saw almost constant defensive fighting on the long Danube frontier, as vast movements of population in the Eurasian hinterland began to force a succession of tribal peoples west and south against Rome's borders. Parthia, later Sassanid Persia, made equally frequent attempts on the Caucasian and Mesopotamian fronts.

The late 3rd Century Illyrian soldier-emperors achieved an extraordinary, if partial military recovery from the 260s AD onwards; and in the 280s and 330s two emperors of genius, Diocletianus and Constantinus, virtually redesigned the Roman state. But it was a relatively impoverished and demoralised state, which was only rebuilt at the cost of totalitarian regime; an intrusive and costly bureaucracy ruinous taxes and merciless conscription did not comman willing loyalty. The old Roman values of duty and discipline characteristic of the years of optimistic expansion, had bee leached away. The old certainties - the authority of th monarchy, a vibrant economy, military loyalty and the hab of victory - had all been destroyed; they could only b restored in fragile imitation.

As the 4th Century wore on the new mobile reserve devised by Diocletianus proved unable to prevent th barbarians from raging through the frontier provinces eve few years - while human greed usually sabotaged h theoretically admirable pattern for an orderly succession c emperors. Each defeat, each tide of raiders cost mor irreplaceable men and gold, and further damaged th dwindling resources of the state. Each mutiny, each blood squabble over the diminished throne cost more in hop belief and prestige. By the end of the century the names of few of the old legions were all that was remembered in c army which had utterly changed character.

The dread of Rome's name could no longer hold back c entire continent on the move. The catastrophe c Hadrianopolis, in 378, was the fatal wound. For another thir years Roman armies, scraped together as much from ha disciplined barbarian mercenaries as from branded provinci conscripts, scrambled back and forth between the Rhine an Thrace, commanded more loyally by the Vandal warlor Stilicho than by rival Roman generals. But in the first years the 5th Century the dams were finally swept away; German tribesmen beyond numbering poured over the Rhine, acro Gaul and Spain, even crossing to North Africa; and in 410 A Rome herself was contemptuously sacked by her one-tim paid ally, Alaric the Goth. The Roman Empire in the West wc gone forever.

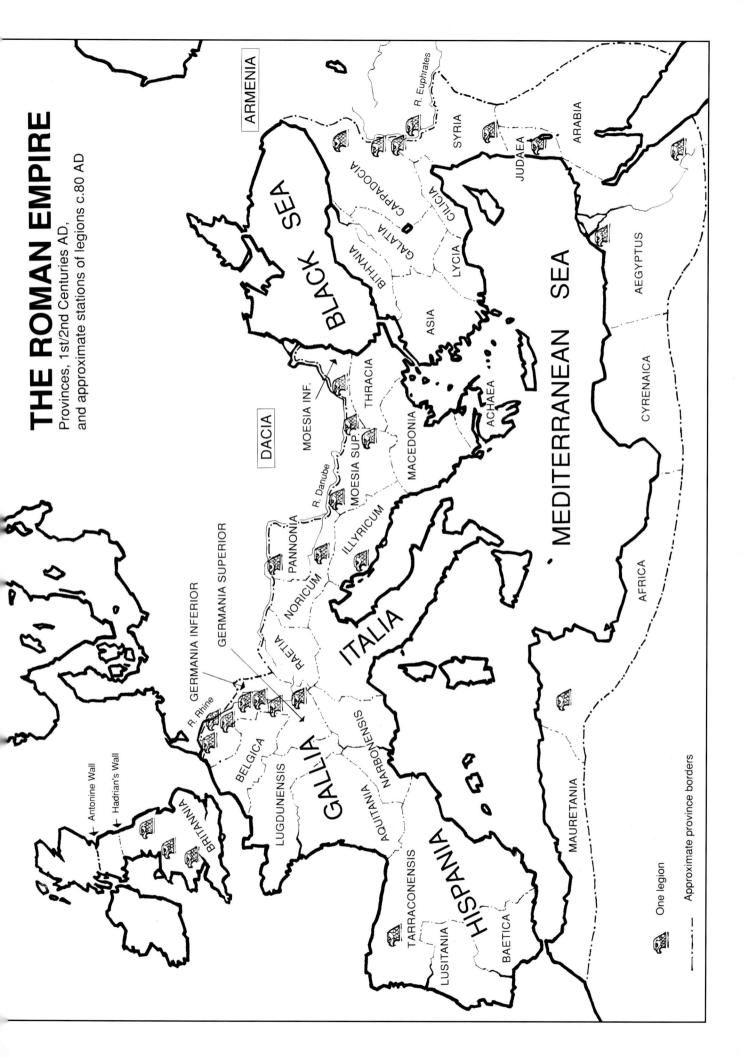

THE ROMAN EMPIRE

Provinces, 1st/2nd Centuries AD,
and approximate stations of legions c.80 AD

ARMENIA

DACIA

BLACK SEA

MEDITERRANEAN SEA

SYRIA

ARABIA

JUDAEA

AEGYPTUS

CYRENAICA

CAPPADOCIA

GALATIA

BITHYNIA

LYCIA

CILICIA

ASIA

ACHAEA

MACEDONIA

THRACIA

MOESIA INF.

R. Euphrates

R. Danube

MOESIA SUP.

ILLYRICUM

PANNONIA

NORICUM

RAETIA

GERMANIA SUPERIOR

GERMANIA INFERIOR

R. Rhine

BELGICA

LUGDUNENSIS

GALLIA

AQUITANIA

NARBONENSIS

ITALIA

AFRICA

MAURETANIA

HISPANIA

BAETICA

LUSITANIA

TARRACONENSIS

BRITANNIA

Antonine Wall

Hadrian's Wall

One legion

Approximate province borders

ROMAN FRONTIER FORT

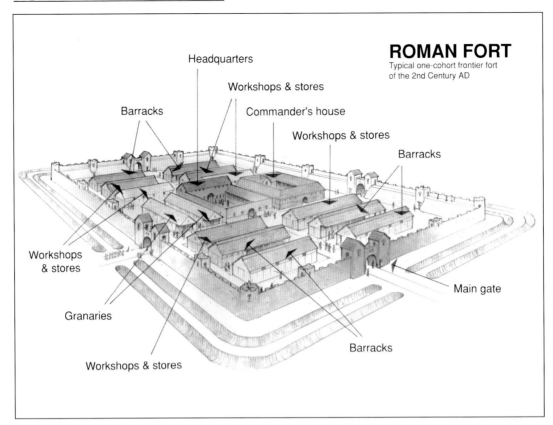

ROMAN FORT
Typical one-cohort frontier fort
of the 2nd Century AD

Headquarters

Workshops & stores

Commander's house

Barracks

Workshops & stores

Barracks

Workshops & stores

Barracks

Main gate

Granaries

Workshops & stores

Barracks

During campaigns of expansion Roman armies built forts of turf and timber to guard the limits of each new advance, to protect lines of communication through newly occupied tribal areas, and to accomodate troops lying up for the winter. As the frontiers moved forward these might be abandoned or destroyed, or they might be permanently garrisoned. The traces of hundreds of such posts have been located.

Their defences were adequate, but not massive: they were essentially bases from which troops moved out to fight offensively in the open. Although some sites do betray signs of having been stormed and burnt by the tribes during major outbreaks, forts were normally safe against enemies lacking siege technology. Depending on the terrain they might be surrounded by one, two, or more ditches, carefully sited and profiled to trap attackers in a "killing ground" within javelin-throw of the ramparts.

As some frontiers solidified into permanent defensive borders in the 2nd Century, old forts were strengthened with stone ramparts, and new posts were built in stone. Archaeology suggests that it was common for the facing wall of the ramparts, the gatehouses and rampart towers, the headquarters building, the commander's house and perhaps the granaries to be built in stone, while the barracks and miscellaneous stores and workshops often remained in timber or plastered wattle on stone footings. Some forts were occupied, continually or at intervals, for centuries; many sites show evidence of periodic improvement, re-occupation or rebuilding. A few have revealed the addition of artillery platforms behind the rampart-walk, to support catapults; these ominous reminders of the increased threat of direct attack usually date from the 3rd Century.

Frontier forts varied in size and internal layout according to the garrison (between about 3.75 acres for an infantry cohort, and 12.5 acres for a cavalry *ala milliaria*); and in exact shape according to the terrain; but our drawing shows a "typical" playing card-shaped single cohort post with stone defences, to accomodate an auxiliary cohort of about 48? men. Such forts were usually sited within a day's easy marc of one another for mutual support, and linked by good road with small signal-relay stations (apparently for passing smok and fire signals) at shorter intervals. Inscriptions suggest the garrison units might sometimes occupy the same post f many decades.

The exact layout of the barracks, stores and workshops the "corners" varied widely, but certain features are almo invariably found. The road from the main gate leads direc to a central headquarters building, beside which is th commander's imposing house; and continues behind it to th rear gate. A crossways road links the side gates, passir across the front of the HQ building and commander's hous Granaries, with buttressed walls and raised floors, were usua sited centrally, with easy wagon access to a gate.

The HQ building had a colonnaded courtyard, often w a well or water tanks, flanked by ranges of rooms believed have housed the central armoury. At the rear was a impressive two-storey-high hall with a dais at one en presumably for indoor ceremonial; along its rear side we ranged offices, the paymaster's strongroom, etc., centred the shrine where the unit standards and other religious objec were housed.

Fort sites have yielded evidence for fairly sophisticate water supply and sewerage arrangements, including latri blocks cleaned by running water. The purpose of many of th interior buildings is unknown, however; the siting of the stab in cavalry forts is not yet fully understood, and as mention under Plate 14, no central cooking or messing arrangemer have been identified. In fact, surprisingly few of the hundre of known fort sites have been thoroughly excavate particularly with regard to internal buildings apart from t central range; future generations of historians have mu enjoyable work to do.

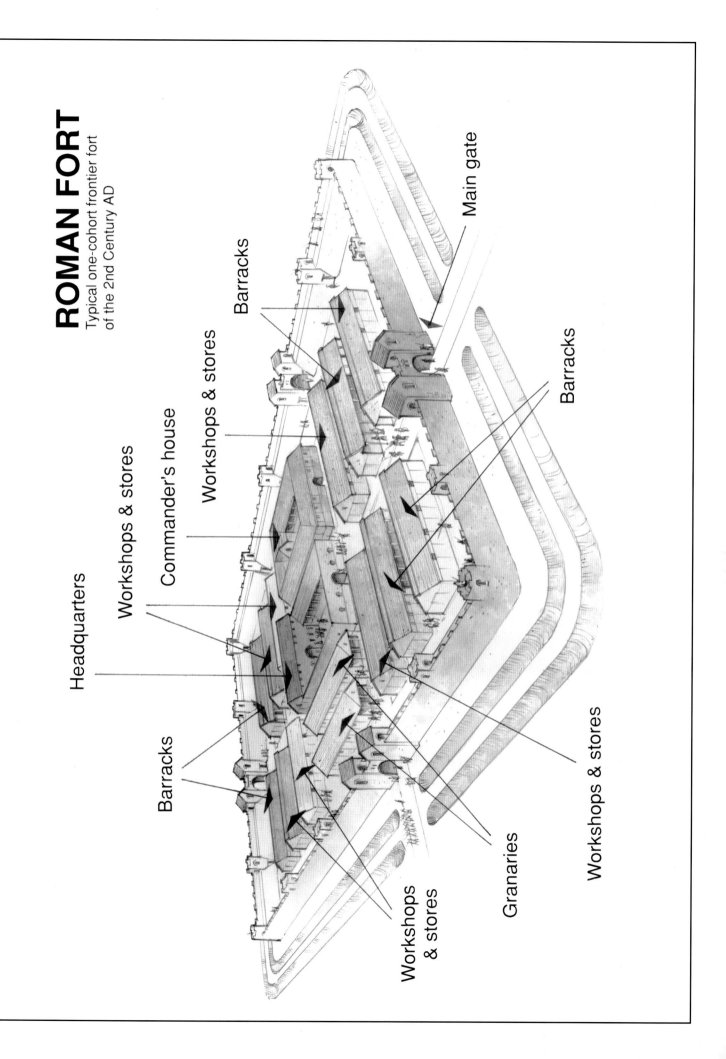

ROMAN FORT
Typical one-cohort frontier fort
of the 2nd Century AD

Headquarters

Workshops & stores

Commander's house

Workshops & stores

Barracks

Main gate

Barracks

Barracks

Workshops & stores

Granaries

Workshops & stores